Presented to

_____

by

_____

on

_____

A CHILD'S FIRST BIBLE

A CHILD'S FIRST BEDTIME PRAYERS

25 Heart-to-Heart Talks with JESUS

written by Dandi Daley Mackall | illustrated by Cee Biscoe

 TYNDALE KIDS

Tyndale House Publishers
Carol Stream, Illinois

For Harper and Madison—Jesus loves YOU!

Visit Tyndale's website for kids at tyndale.com/kids.

Visit Dandi Daley Mackall online at dandibooks.com.

Tyndale is a registered trademark of Tyndale House Ministries. The Tyndale Kids logo is a trademark of Tyndale House Ministries.

A Child's First Bedtime Prayers

Copyright © 2022 by Dandi A. Mackall. All rights reserved.

Illustrations by Cee Biscoe. Copyright © Tyndale House Ministries. All rights reserved.

Designed by Julie Chen

Edited by Deborah King

Unless otherwise indicated, all Scripture quotations are taken from the *Holy Bible*, New Living Translation, copyright © 1996, 2004, 2015 by Tyndale House Foundation. Used by permission of Tyndale House Publishers, Carol Stream, Illinois 60188. All rights reserved.

Scripture quotations marked TLB are taken from *The Living Bible*, copyright © 1971 by Tyndale House Foundation. Used by permission of Tyndale House Publishers, Carol Stream, Illinois 60188. All rights reserved.

For manufacturing information regarding this product, please call 1-855-277-9400.

For information about special discounts for bulk purchases, please contact Tyndale House Publishers at csresponse@tyndale.com, or call 1-855-277-9400.

Library of Congress Cataloging-in-Publication Data

A catalog record for this book is available from the Library of Congress.

ISBN 978-1-4964-5421-8

Printed in China

28	27	26	25	24	23	22
7	6	5	4	3	2	1

Contents

Introduction

I REMEMBER SAYING MY PRAYERS WHEN I WAS A CHILD. Usually, the prayers were ones my sister and I had memorized from simple repetition:

> *Thank you for the food we eat.*
> *Thank you, God, for food so sweet.*
> *Bless this food which we're about to eat*
> *and the hands that prepared it.*
> *Be present at our table, Lord.*
> *Be here and everywhere adored.*

At night, I'd thank God for that day (even if it was a crummy one) and ask him to bless everybody and every pet. I got to stay up later that way.

I never expected God to talk back. I suspect I said those prayers as much for my parents as for God.

Only years later, after I had become a Christian and understood the love and grace of our heavenly Father, did I realize God wanted me to talk to him—really talk, even if the words didn't rhyme, even if the thoughts swirled unformed from my cluttered head. And as I began reading, then studying, the Scriptures, I understood that God, through Jesus, had opened a two-way passage of communication. I could actually have heart-to-hearts with Jesus. He offers such an unimaginable privilege to us every minute of every day.

I've written this book prayerfully. In each of these heartfelt, childlike talks, the child prays to Jesus, and Jesus answers. I've done my best to base every response on specific verses from the Word of God, where God really does speak to us. Please check out additional Bible verses for each prayer at firstbedtimeprayers.com.

My prayer is that your family will draw closer to Jesus as you talk . . . and listen . . . in bedtime prayers.

Dandi Daley Mackall

Come close to God, and God will come close to you.
JAMES 4:8

Because he bends down to listen,
I will pray as long as I have breath!
PSALM 116:2

Let's Talk

Dear Jesus,

I like saying prayers, but I'd love something more.
I want to go deeper than ever before.
I'm not great at praying, but you don't keep score.
I'm talking about bedtime prayers.

I always say thank you for Mom and for Dad,
For Grammy and Grandpa and friends that I've had.
But is it okay if I'm sad or I'm mad,
To say all I feel in my prayers?

Sometimes I pray, but my heart isn't there.
I say the right words in a not-thinking prayer.
I say the words fast, without being aware
That you're really hearing my prayers.

You're awfully big. You can see that I'm small.
So why should you bother to answer at all?
But I'd like to pray. Am I hearing your call
To know you in great bedtime prayers?

Dear Child,

Before you were born, long before you could walk,
I knew you and loved you and wanted to talk.
I stand at your door. You are hearing me knock.
I'll join you in close bedtime prayers!

I'm soft as your blankie. I'm safe as your Gram.
You know I'm your Shepherd, and you are my lamb.
You wanted to talk, and, my love, here I am!
I'll lead you in great bedtime prayers.

I open my arms. Come and sit on my knee!
I welcome you, child, to be all you can be.
Just climb in my lap and keep talking with me.
We'll cuddle for great bedtime prayers!

Look! I stand at the door and knock. If you hear
my voice and open the door, I will come in,
and we will share a meal together as friends.

REVELATION 3:20

Imagine you're sitting on Jesus' lap.
Is there anything you'd like to talk
over with him right now?

Why Do I Have Bedtime?

Dear Jesus,

Daddy says it's time for bed.
Mom calls me a sleepyhead.
How about a snack instead?
Why do I have bedtime?

"Time to put your toys away."
"Time to sleep now. No more play."
Why not have a longer day
And stay awake at bedtime?

I don't want to go to sleep!
You won't catch me counting sheep.
Give me daylight I can keep.
I really don't need bedtime.

Dear Child,

I'm thankful for your daytime praise,
But if I only made you days,
You'd miss the nighttime giveaways,
Like peace and rest and sleep.

See the moon shine silvery light?
I can speak through stars so bright.
Come on now! You know I'm right.
Let's snuggle down to sleep.

Every night you need your rest.
Your Creator knows you best.
Close your eyes, and don't protest.
It's time for you to sleep.

For me, the best is when we meet,
When busy daytime's all complete.
Your bedtime prayers are super sweet.
Now take my gift of sleep.

Dear Jesus,

Thanks for answering. You're so right!
Now the sun is out of sight.
Time for bed, Lord. Nighty-night.
I think I'll go to sleep.

God gives rest to his loved ones.

PSALM 127:2

Why do you think you have to go to bed at night?

Best Friends Forever

Dear Jesus,

You're so big, and I'm so small.
I'M confused. YOU know it all.
I cry out. You hear my call.
Could you be my friend?

If other kids say, "Go away!
You're no friend, so you can't play,"
Everything will be okay
If you and I are friends.

You're my God, and you're my King.
You created everything.
I can hide beneath your wing.
Will you be my friend?

Dear Child,

I am friends with girls and guys—
Every color, shape, and size.
Some are funny. Some are wise.
I'd LOVE to be your friend!

Other friends may turn on you.
Once, a friend betrayed me, too.
I know what you're going through.
I'll always be your friend.

Here it is, my guarantee:
BFFs? That's you and me!
Now and through eternity,
I promise we'll be friends.

Dear Jesus,

I could whisper; I could shout.
You will never leave me out!
Jesus, I will never doubt
That you and I are friends!

God will surely do this for you, for he always does just what he says, and he is the one who invited you into this wonderful friendship with his Son, even Christ our Lord.

1 CORINTHIANS 1:9, TLB

What makes someone a best friend, and how can you be best friends with Jesus?

You Keep Me Safe

Dear Jesus,

I sure don't like to be afraid,
Like when I saw that big parade,
Or heard the roar that lion made
When we were at the zoo.

Strangers, dogs, and too-loud noise,
Bigger girls and bigger boys,
Even certain crazy toys
Can make me feel unsafe.

Underwater's awfully scary!
Cats can scratch or be too hairy.
I steer clear of our canary.
Jesus, keep me safe!

Dear child,

When you're frightened, think of me.
I'm right here, and that's the key.
Little one, I guarantee:
I'll always keep you safe.

Next time, when you start to fear,
Don't forget that I am near.
Talk to me—I always hear.
And I will keep you safe.

Even when I walk through the darkest valley, I will not be afraid, for you are close beside me.

PSALM 23:4

*What will you do
the next time you're frightened?*

Thanks for Little Things

Dear Jesus,

Thanks for puddles. Thanks for rocks.
Thanks for boots and warm wool socks.
How I love a cardboard box!
Thanks for little things.

Grandpa's wrinkles, Grandma's eyes.
Running, catching fireflies.
Painting faces, cool disguise!
Thanks for little things.

Roly-polies, tiny ants.
New spring leaves from little plants.
Twirling in a silly dance—
Thanks for little things.

Dear child,

I created little things!
Puppy tails and soft moth wings—
Chirping when a robin sings—
I love little things.

Little things bring giant joys!
On the playground, girls and boys
Squeal and laugh—a joyful noise.
Little things are great.

Rainbows when the skies are gray,
Snowflakes on a winter's day,
Funny things your parents say—
Love the little things!

God created everything through him,
and nothing was created except through him.

JOHN 1:3

*What little thing did you enjoy
doing—or seeing—today?*

How Can You Love Me?

Dear Jesus,

How can you love me? You know me too well.
You see me get angry. Then sometimes I yell.
I mess up so often. I know you can tell.
I'm asking, "Lord, how can you love me?"

I'm not always lovable. I can be mean.
I want my own way or I'll make a big scene.
I drew on my walls in bright purple and green.
I'm wondering how you can love me.

I know right from wrong, but I still disobey.
I'm sorry I just think of ME night and day.
You say that you love me. Is love here to stay?
It's hard to believe you still love me.

Dear child,

I hope that you know you were loved from the start.
I'm holding your hand, and I live in your heart.
Now nothing and no one can pull us apart.
Forever and ever I'll love you!

Our Father God loves you. He sent me, his Son!
I died for your sins, and I paid for each one.
My love's not because of the good things you've done.
I love you! I love you! I love you!

I will always trust in God's unfailing love.

PSALM 52:8

How do you know Jesus loves you?
Want to sing "Jesus Loves Me"?

whiter than Snow

Dear Jesus,

Thanks for our snowman! (We made him from snow.)
Super-cool snowflakes, the stars of your show!
You're a great artist! I hope that you know
I'm glad that you sent me your snow.

Glittery snow crunches under my feet,
Piling on hedges and houses and street.
Drifts of white snow make the vision complete.
Look what you did with that snow!

Out back we throw garbage in big plastic bins,
Like rotten potatoes and smelly old skins.
It's dirty and ugly—a lot like our sins—
You cover it all with your snow!

Dear Child,

My snow is a teacher so you can grow wise.
And this is the lesson you must realize:
I died for your sins, and my love beautifies!
I wash your sins whiter than snow.

I've covered each sin—you are totally mine.
And just like the snow, let your life be a sign
That you are my masterpiece! You're my design.
I washed your sins whiter than snow.

"Come now, let's settle this," says the Lord. "Though your sins are like scarlet, I will make them as white as snow. Though they are red like crimson, I will make them as white as wool."

ISAIAH 1:18

Thank Jesus for forgiving you and making you his masterpiece.

8

You Made Me the Way That I Am

Dear Jesus,

My brother is much better looking than me.
My sister is smarter. Just ask her—you'll see.
My friends are all taller—so shouldn't I be?
Why did you make me this way?

I wish I were faster. I'd win every race!
My legs are so short. I am always last place.
So when we play ball, I can't get to first base.
Why did you make me this way?

I don't like my ears, and my head is too flat.
My arms are too skinny. My face is too fat.
I have to wear glasses, so what about that?
Why did you make me this way?

Dear Child,

I'm happy to see that you're honest in prayer!
I knew all your thoughts before you were aware.
It's tempting to envy. It hurts to compare.
But trust me! I made you this way.

If someone is smart, tell me, what's that to you?
You think you're too short? There's not much you can do.
I think you're just right! And I'm telling you true:
I made you the way that you are!

Before you were born,
You were known through and through.
Your parts are designed so there's no one like you.
You're super fantastic from my point of view!
I made you the way that you are.

Thank you for making me so wonderfully complex!
Your workmanship is marvelous—how well I know it.

PSALM 139:14

*What do you like best
about how God made you?*

Thanks for the Animals

Dear Jesus,

Thanks for the sparrow I saw yesterday.
Bluebirds and robins and goldfinch—hurray!
Woodpeckers pecking, then flying away.
Thank you for making the birds.

I hear the cry of a sweet mourning dove.
Honking of geese as they fly up above.
Flapping of wings sounds like feathery love.
Thanks for the sounds of the birds.

You shaped the eels with their wiggly tails.
You formed the fish with their colorful scales.
You made the snails and the squid and the whales!
Thanks for the creatures you made.

What about horses? They prance and look proud.
Lions and leopards with roars extra loud,
Sheep with their wool like a puffy, white cloud.
Thank you for making each one.

Squirrels make me giggle, and deer make me dance.
Skunks, wolves, and foxes, and even the ants—
All would say, "Thank you!" if given the chance.
Thanks for the creatures you made.

Dear child,

I worked with my Father, along with the Spirit.
We laughed making warthogs. Creation could hear it.
The roar of the lion, the lamb curled so near it—
Such fun with the creatures we made!

We sang with the robins, a spring-y sweet song.
The necks of giraffes we made ever so long.
The bears, apes, and oxen, we made them all strong.
Such strength in the creatures we made!

From oceans to sky, we made all of the creatures!
No two are alike, if you study their features.
And some, like the ants, can be hardworking teachers.
I love all the creatures we made!

You care for people and animals alike, O LORD.

PSALM 36:6

What's your favorite animal? Why?

Never Alone

Dear Jesus,

I know that you love me, but days like today,
I can't feel your love. It seems too far away.
I'm lonely and sad, and I'm sorry to say,
I don't feel like talking tonight.

Dear Child,

You know that I love you with all of my heart,
So feel it or not, we are never apart.
I think we should talk, but tonight I can start.
I'm always right here for a talk.

Though sometimes you think that
you're out on your own,
I feel what you feel, and I hear every groan,
But I'm always with you. You're never alone.
Just talk to me, knowing I'm here.

Dear Jesus,

My feelings get crazy, and sometimes they're wrong.
I'll stick to the facts: You are here all day long.
I'm part of your family. That's where I belong.
I know I am never alone.

Dear child,

At bedtime, your prayers can stay locked in your head.
But I know your thoughts long before they are said.
Just whisper my name as you lie on your bed.
Remember: You're never alone.

Be sure of this: I am with you always,
even to the end of the age.

MATTHEW 28:20

*Thank God that you are never, ever
alone because of Jesus.*

Grace over Guilt

Dear Jesus,

I hurt my friend's feelings with words I regret.
She said, "I forgive you," but I can't forget.
So now I feel guilty. I'm down and upset.
How can I live with my guilt?

Guilt feels like a curtain of sadness and pain.
Guilt weighs on my shoulders. It rattles my brain!
I know that I'm guilty. My sin left a stain.
When will my guilt go away?

Dear Child,

It's good to be sorry for things you do wrong.
Just ask for forgiveness. It doesn't take long.
Accept what I promise. Then move right along.
My grace is far greater than guilt.

I paid for your sins when I died on the Cross.
I say you're forgiven, and I am the boss!
To fail to believe this would be such a loss!
My grace covers all of your guilt.

Your guilt can appear as an unwelcome guest.
It might try to stay, even once you've confessed.
But I remove sin far as east is from west!
My grace takes your sin far away.

Your sins and your deeds, I'll remember no more.
I choose to forget, and I'm not keeping score.
Just knock, knock, knock, knock! I will open the door.
My grace wipes away all your guilt.

Dear Jesus,

I thank you, my Savior! I'm so glad you came.
Whenever I'm feeling my guilt and my shame,
I'll thank you for grace, and I'll call out your name.
Thank you for taking my guilt.

He has removed our sins as far from us
as the east is from the west.

PSALM 103:12

*What should you do when you feel
guilty about something?*

Thanks for Colors

Dear Jesus,

Tell me how you thought of green—
Light green, dark green, in between.
Did you have a green machine?
Thanks for making green.

I'd sure miss that bright blue sky,
Bluebells, bluebirds flying by.
No blue oceans? I might cry!
Thanks for making blue.

Red-winged blackbirds, cardinal flocks—
Scarlet beetles, reddish fox—
Red at sunset, roses, rocks—
Thanks for making red.

Purple berries, yellow sun—
Orange and pink are so much fun.
Rainbow colors on the run!
Thanks for making colors!

Dear Child,

If the world were black and white,
Daytime might look just like night.
Colors make an awesome sight!
Glad you like my colors.

All the colors of creation
Bless the folks of every nation.
Colors are a celebration!
Glad you like my colors!

The earth . . . is robed in brilliant colors.

JOB 38:14

What's your favorite color?
What animals are that color?

NO AnSwers

Dear Jesus,

I wanted a puppy with curls and a bow.
I prayed and I prayed, but your answer was NO.
I don't have a puppy, so I'd like to know,
Why won't you answer my prayers?

I know you created all birds in the air,
Each bunny, each beaver, each bat, bull, and bear.
I just want one puppy. Could you and I share?
Why do you keep saying NO?

Dear Child,

Your prayer may be answered with YES or with NO,
Or MAYBE or WAIT. (And that answer feels slow!)
You might understand, or you may never know.
Just trust that I answer with love.

You know I could give you all things that you wish:
A roomful of monkeys, a bathtub of fish.
Enough scoops of ice cream to fill every dish!
I'll give you the answer you need.

Dear Jesus,

I prayed for a tree house when I was just three,
I picked out a spot in the tallest oak tree.
And now that I'm older, I guess I can see
The reason your answer was NO.

So thanks for your WAITS and your NOS and the rest.
Deep down I do know that your answer is best.
I'd sure like that puppy, but I am still blessed.
And YES, I'll keep praying to you!

Just as the heavens are higher than the earth,
so my ways are higher than your ways and
my thoughts higher than your thoughts.

ISAIAH 55:9

*Have you ever prayed
for something that you didn't get?*

A Family of Thank-Yous

Dear Jesus,

Cocoa in my favorite mug,
Feeling Daddy's giant hug,
Kneeling on my bedroom rug—
Thank you for my daddy.

On a hillside smelling flowers,
Gramps and I watch clouds for hours,
Finding castles, knights, and towers.
Thank you for my grandpa.

Mommy's laugh—I love her smile—
Giggling when we walk a mile,
Stopping just to talk awhile—
Thank you for my mommy.

Squishy mud between my toes,
Chocolate pudding on my nose,
Wind, a kite, and there it goes!
Thank you for my grandma.

Curled up in my special nook,
Listening to my favorite book,
Love is everywhere I look—
Thank you for my family.

Fuzzy, tickly Teddy Bear,
Piles of pillows everywhere,
Knowing that you're always there—
I just want to thank you.

Dear Child,

Being grateful pleases me.
Giving thanks can help you see
People in YOUR family
Are special gifts from God!

God decided in advance to adopt us
into his own family by bringing us to himself
through Jesus Christ. This is what he wanted
to do, and it gave him great pleasure.

EPHESIANS 1:5

*Why do you think God gave you
each member of your family?*

Night Watch

Dear Jesus,

When it's time to go to sleep,
Noises creak, and shadows creep.
Outside, cars scream *Beep! Beep! Beep!*
Jesus, are you watching?

Dear Child,

Trust in me and go to bed.
You'll be safe from toe to head.
I will guard you, as I've said,
"I am always watching."

Dear Jesus,

What if you get sleepy too?
What's a kid like me to do?
If I call or cry for you,
Jesus, will you hear me?

Dear Child,

I never ever shut my eyes.
I'm always close to hear your cries.
So listen for my lullabies.
I am always listening.

Dear Jesus,

Thank you, Jesus! I'm all right.
I don't even need a light.
Getting sleepy . . . nighty-night.
Thanks for always watching.

I lay down and slept, yet I woke up in safety,
for the Lord was watching over me.

PSALM 3:5

Thank Jesus for always watching over you.

No Fair

Dear Jesus,

Last night at supper, my feelings got hurt.
Mom gave my brother the biggest dessert.
Brother said, "Your piece is small like you, Squirt."
I don't think that's very fair.

Here is another thing I find unfair.
My sister can fix her own long, curly hair.
Whenever I fix mine, kids laugh as they stare.
How is that possibly fair?

When playing a game, it's a sure thing I'll lose.
When choosing up teams, I'm the last one they choose.
And sometimes I can't even tie my own shoes.
That doesn't seem very fair.

Dear child,

I see what you mean, and I know you're upset.
Your future's ahead, so please, never forget:
I made you my own, and I'm not finished yet.
I am good, and my goodness is fair.

I gave you your life, and I gave you mine too.
Now that wasn't fair, but I did it for you.
You're loved and forgiven whatever you do.
I am good. You're my child, and I'm good.

Dear Jesus,

I know that you're right, and I see I was wrong.
And when I am weak, I can feel that you're strong.
I'll drift off to sleep, and I'll sing a new song:
You are good, and I know you are fair.

We know that God causes everything to work together for the good of those who love God and are called according to his purpose for them.

ROMANS 8:28

What are some ways God has been good to you?

Everyday Praise

Dear Jesus,

On Sunday at church when they talk about praise,
I think of my granny—her whole body sways.
They say I can praise you in all sorts of ways.
But, Lord, I don't know how to praise.

My daddy finds praise in the Twenty-third Psalm.
My mama sings hymns, and they make her look calm,
As if she's at peace in your heavenly palm.
But, Jesus, I can't seem to praise.

I'm nervous on Sundays. Does praise have commands?
I'm not really sure what to do with my hands.
I smile at our pastor—hope he understands.
I really don't know how to praise.

Dear child,

It does my heart good that you're thinking of this.
When aiming to praise, there's no way you can miss.
And praise from the heart, well, it feels like a kiss.
Come closer in everyday praise.

You don't have to praise me just one day a week!
The earth's filled with praise if you're willing to seek.
Just tell me what's awesome, what's cool—so to speak—
And soon you'll be bursting with praise!

At times it's the big things—like stars, moon, and sky.
At times it's the small things—the wings of a fly,
A hummingbird's hum, or a sweet lullaby.
Let everyday gifts stir up praise.

Dear Jesus,

A cardinal flies in a rich splash of red.
A mourning dove cries, and I feel what it said.
The smell of the dawn can go straight to my head.
Is that what you mean by a praise?

Cracks in the sidewalk where flowers still grow.
Laughter and giggles as soft as the snow.
Praising in whispers, I'll say, "Way to go!"
And I can keep going with praise!

My new baby sister is learning to smile.
I'm grateful to you as I watch her awhile.
I have to confess, Lord, I sure like your style!
You're always so worthy of praise!

I will praise you, Lord, with all my heart;
I will tell of all the marvelous things you have done.

PSALM 9:1

What did you notice that made you smile
or reminded you of God today?

Self-Control Goal

Dear Jesus,

Today I got thoughts I don't want in my head.
My sis made me angry, then full speed ahead,
I said something mean that I shouldn't have said.
Lord Jesus, I need self-control.

I once shoved a boy so I'd be first in line.
I grabbed the last cookie and shouted, "All mine!"
And when I want more, then I cry, or I whine.
You see how I need self-control?

I'd sit on my hands, but that gets pretty sore.
I'm out of control, so I need a lot more.
I can't buy control in a grocery store.
Lord, where can I get self-control?

I try and I try, but it does me no good.
I can't shut my mouth when I know that I should.
What's wrong with me, Jesus? I wish that I could
Go find me some more self-control.

Dear Child,

I know it's not easy to have self-control.
So think about me in your heart and your soul.
Together we'll conquer your self-control goal.
I'll help you to find self-control.

Come quickly to me before starting a fight.
I'm here for a talk and to make things all right.
Rely on the Spirit by day and by night.
Together we'll find self-control.

The Holy Spirit produces this kind of fruit in our
lives: love, joy, peace, patience, kindness, goodness,
faithfulness, gentleness, and self-control.

GALATIANS 5:22-23

*What can make you lose control and say
or do something you shouldn't?*

Sleepyhead Prayer

Dear Jesus,

Just me, Jesus, here to pray.
Bestest way to end my day.
I have lots and lots to say,
But I am getting sleepy.

Countless gifts to thank you for:
Horses, birds, and so much more.
Dogs and cats (and I have four).
But I am getting sleepy.

Gran and Grandpa, cousins too.
Even brothers—I've got two!
Green, green trees, a sky so blue.
But I am really sleepy.

Dear Child,

How I love to hear you pray!
Here's a thought: It's A-OK
To talk to me throughout the day.
I know you're getting sleepy.

In the morning I'll be here.
Chat with me, or give a cheer!
Afternoons, you know I'm near,
You won't be quite as sleepy.

How I yearn to talk with you
Late at night, but daytime too,
Even when there's nothing new.
So, sleepyhead, good night.

Never stop praying.

1 THESSALONIANS 5:17

*When could you talk to God
during the day tomorrow?*

Thanks for Funny

Dear Jesus,

My daddy told a silly joke.
I laughed so hard I thought I'd choke.
My puppy licked me when I woke.
Jesus, thanks for funny.

I love to tumble down the hill.
It makes me feel like Jack or Jill—
All dizzy even standing still.
Jesus, thanks for funny.

Splashing on a day that's sunny—
Giggling when I see a bunny—
I know you created funny.
Jesus, thanks for funny.

Dear child,

Children sitting on my knee,
Playing games in Galilee,
Sometimes things you say to me
Are wonderful and funny.

Peek-a-boo, a kangaroo,
Laughter, when it comes from you,
Fills my heart with laughter too.
It's great that you love funny!

We were filled with laughter, and we sang for joy.
And the other nations said, "What amazing
things the Lord has done for them."

PSALM 126:2

What makes you laugh?

You Do Care

Dear Jesus,

Today was so sad that I cried and I cried.
Lord, how could this happen? I'm broken inside.
I cared for my fish, but my fishy still died.
How could you let my pet die?

Dear child,

I love you, my child, and I'm sad when you're sad.
I cry when you cry, and I hurt when you're mad.
But things in this life can be both good and bad.
Let's talk all about your pet fish.

Dear Jesus,

The day that I got him, my fish made me smile.
I stared and I stared at my fish for a while.
I thanked you and praised you and named my fish Kyle.
Why did my fish have to die?

The first thing I did when I woke up each day
Was feed little Kyle and then watch my fish play.
Lord, is it my fault that my pet's not okay?
Why did my fish have to die?

I know that my fish was the bestest one ever.
Dear Kyle was so funny, and swimmy, and clever.
My dad said, "A new fish?" But I told him, "Never!"
Why did my fish have to die?

I feel all alone since I lost my sweet pet.
My fishbowl is empty, the glass barely wet.
I wonder, dear Lord, will I ever forget?
Do you care that my fishy-fish died?

Dear child,

I care when a sparrow falls down from the sky.
I know that it hurts when your favorite pets die.
But one day I'll wipe every tear from your eye.
I'll comfort you now with my love.

I won't allow sorrow that you cannot bear.
So climb in my lap, and I'll comfort you there.
Then take in my love like a breath of fresh air.
We'll share all our memories of Kyle.

Dear Jesus,

I thank you for listening when I get upset.
I know that you know I'm not over this yet.
But you're the Creator, and you made my pet.
You cared for my fishy and me.

He will wipe every tear from their eyes, and there will be no more death or sorrow or crying or pain. All these things are gone forever.

REVELATION 21:4

When you're sad, how does Jesus make you feel better?

I Can't See You

Dear Jesus,

I'm not very sleepy, and something's not right.
I wish you felt closer, but you're out of sight.
Lord, how can I find you? I need you tonight.
I wish I could see you right now.

I wish I could hear you, your booming loud voice.
I'd ask you to sing me a song of your choice.
Your words in the Bible can help me rejoice,
But I wish I could hear you right now.

I know your disciples were able to see
The smile on your face as you calmed the wild sea.
I'm asking, dear Lord, if you'd do that for me.
I wish I could see you right now.

Dear child,

You can't see the wind, but you see where it blows.
The leaves fall from trees. The wind tickles your nose.
It's here, then it's gone. No one knows where it goes.
Like the wind, I am here with you now.

Believe without seeing. Your faith multiplies!
I give you my promise, and I don't tell lies.
Remember to look with your heart, not your eyes.
You will see I'm right here with you now.

Dear Jesus,

Lord Jesus, I see you—down deep in my heart.
I'm sorry I doubted. That wasn't so smart.
You're always nearby—that's the very best part!
I believe you are here with me now.

Jesus told him, "You believe because you have seen me. Blessed are those who believe without seeing me."

JOHN 20:29

Do you believe you will see Jesus one day?

People I Don't Know

Dear Jesus,

I'm thinking of people I might never meet,
Like families too poor to buy something to eat,
The sick and the homeless who sleep in the street.
I pray that you'll help them tonight.

I'm thinking of people that I've never met.
Lord, what if they're frightened or very upset?
Please help all those people who don't know you yet.
I pray they will come to you, Lord.

For kids who have birthdays, but never get cake,
Please help them to see all the blessings you make,
Like trees, and the sky, and the sun on a lake.
I'll pray they receive all your gifts.

I've heard about countries where Christians are banned.
They're sharing the gospel 'cause that's your command.
They're thrown into jails just for taking a stand!
Please help those believers in jail.

I pray for the lady who lives right next door.
And please help the man at the grocery store.
Policemen and teachers and so many more—
Please help me remember to pray.

Dear child,

I want you to pray, and I'm happy you care!
When people are hurting, I'll always be there.
Keep praying for people in need everywhere.
I know them, and I love them too!

I urge you, first of all, to pray for all people. Ask God to help them; intercede on their behalf, and give thanks for them.

1 TIMOTHY 2:1

What could you pray for people in other countries?

Your Peace

Dear Jesus,

I can't get to sleep, Lord. My eyes won't stay shut.
My mom says, "Be calm." I am anything but!
I'm twitchy and feel like my mind's in a rut.
Jesus, please give me your peace.

My belly is squirmy, and sometimes it's ick.
And what's gonna happen if I get real sick?
I'm starting to worry. I need some peace quick.
Jesus, please give me your peace.

I think I hear thunder, so lightning is near!
A storm's on the way, and I'm filling with fear.
What happened to peace? Did it all disappear?
Lord Jesus, I need your peace NOW!

You gave me your peace on the day that we met.
Well, now I'm so restless, I'm starting to sweat.
And Jesus, your peace hasn't made it here yet.
Won't you please give me your peace?

Dear Child,

My peace is right here if you're willing to see.
The way you find peace is by searching for me.
And I'll never leave you. I'm near as can be.
You'll always find peace here with me.

Dear Jesus,

That's right! You're my peace, and I almost forgot.
I'll talk to you, Lord, 'cause you're right on the spot.
I'm better already, so thank you a lot.
Thank you for giving me peace!

I am leaving you with a gift—peace of mind and heart.
And the peace I give is a gift the world cannot give.
So don't be troubled or afraid.

JOHN 14:27

*What does it feel like
when you are peaceful?*

Thanks for You, Jesus!

Dear Jesus,

Now I lay me down to sleep.
There's no sense in counting sheep.
I'll count blessings in a heap.
Thank you for your blessings.

In my heart, you sing a song.
And you love me, right or wrong.
Only you can make me strong.
Jesus, thanks for strength.

Every night you hear my prayer.
All day long, I know you're there.
You go with me everywhere.
Thanks for staying, Jesus.

Best of all, you took my sin,
Gave me grace and peace within.
When I asked, you came right in!
Thank you for salvation!

Thank you for the things you do.
Jesus, I believe in you.
Deep inside, I feel brand new.
Jesus, thanks for YOU!

Dear Child,

You're my child, so celebrate!
You'll love heaven! Heaven's great!
But for now, it's getting late.
Thanks for bedtime prayers!

This is what God has testified: He has given us eternal life, and this life is in his Son.

1 JOHN 5:11

*Thank Jesus for loving you so much
and for living inside you.*

About the Author

DANDI DALEY MACKALL is the award-winning author of about 500 books for children and adults. She visits countless schools, conducts writing assemblies and workshops across the United States, and presents keynote addresses at conferences and events for young authors. She is also a frequent guest on radio talk shows and has made dozens of appearances on TV. She has won several awards for her writing, including the Helen Keating Ott Award for Outstanding Contribution to Children's Literature and the Edgar Award, and is a two-time winner of the Christian Book Award and the Mom's Choice Award.

Dandi writes from rural Ohio, where she lives with her husband, surrounded by their three children, four granddaughters, and a host of animals.

Visit her at DandiBooks.com
and www.facebook.com/dandi.mackall.

Wow! Your Kids with God's Good News!

Teach kids the gospel using four everyday words.

Wow! The Good News in Four Words picture book

Wow! The Good News Tract
Packs of 20

Find free resources, including finger puppets and memory verse cards, at www.tyndal.es/wow.

Grow a lifelong love of God's Word with A Child's First Bible line.

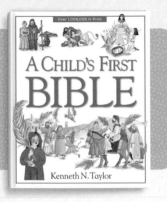

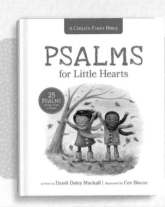

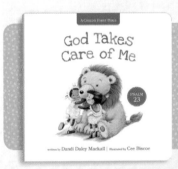

The *God Takes Care of Me* and *God Is Always with Me* board books reveal the deep love and care of our ever-present Father to little ones.

As little learners begin to read, they'll love exploring God's Word on their own with *Psalms for Little Hearts* and the bestselling *A Child's First Bible*.

www.tyndalekids.com

CP1444

Grow a lifelong love of God's Word with A Child's First Bible line.

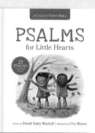

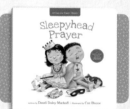

Plant seeds of faith and instill a love of prayer in little ones with the *God Is Always with Me*, *God Takes Care of Me*, *Thanks for Little Things*, and *Sleepyhead Prayer* board books.

As little learners begin to read, they'll love exploring God's Word on their own with *Psalms for Little Hearts*, *A Child's First Bedtime Prayers*, and the bestselling *A Child's First Bible*.

tyndalekids.com

A Perfect Reminder to Cherish All the Milestones—Both the Firsts and the Lasts

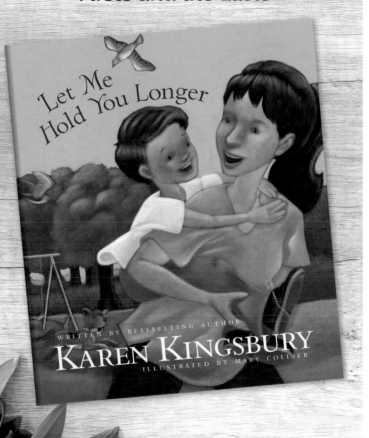

Sweet books to read while you snuggle with your little ones.

tyndalekids.com